WHY I AM A JEW

Printed in Great Britain by The Fanfare Press, London

WHY I AM A JEW

BY EDMOND FLEG

translated by Victor Gollancz

FOR MY GRANDSON
WHO IS NOT YET BORN
E. F.

LONDON
VICTOR GOLLANCZ LTD
1943

CONTENTS

FOREWORD

EDMOND FLEG wrote this proud and humble little book in 1927. It brings now, after sixteen years of anguish for so many peoples, an urgent message of hope and obligation to the Jew, and an urgent call for understanding to the Gentile. Especially, perhaps, will it move those who, in this fifth year of the war, feel themselves, as Fleg would say, " Jewish, very Jewish, but also very English", and, over and above that, simply members of the human community.

A friend has suggested that, being both translator and publisher, I identify myself in a particularly close way with the book (which is indeed my intention) and that I ought therefore to say whether I agree with the whole of it. I would answer that, while it is the noblest exposition of Judaism and what is called " Jewishness " that has come my way, there are a few passages, and one or two of capital importance, with which I am not in agreement. I beg that this personal word may be excused.

I wish to thank the Chief Rabbi, Viola Garvin, and Alan Thomas for their great kindness in reading the translation for me. I cannot adequately express my gratitude to William Pickles, who with a rare graciousness made me free of his scholarship and his sensitive understanding. But most of all would I thank my partner Sheila Hodges, not only for many very valuable suggestions, but, no less, for services rendered during the spring and summer of 1943 which, happily, I cannot attempt to repay.

Fleg dedicated the book to his unborn grandson : no grandson will be born to him, for both his sons died, in the early days of the war, for love of France. The book also carries in itself a broader dedication, a dedication to every Jew of every country in these days of special anxiety and pain. It would be impertinent of me to interpose. But I may be allowed to offer the work of mere translation to the memory of my father, a man of simple honour whom I failed to understand ; and also to a Jewish woman, one of those of whom it was written " Blessed are the pure in heart, for they shall see God."

V. G.

Brimpton, October 8th, 1943

WHY I AM A JEW

People ask me why I am a Jew. It is to you that I want to answer, little unborn grandson.

When will you be old enough to listen to me? My elder son is nineteen, the younger fourteen. When will you be born? Perhaps in ten years' time, perhaps in fifteen. When will you read what I am writing? In 1950 or thereabouts? In 1960? Will anybody be reading in 1960? What will the world look like then? Will the machine have killed the soul? Will the mind have created for itself a new universe? Will the problems that trouble me today mean anything to you? Will there still be Jews?

I believe there will. They have survived the Pharaohs, Nebuchadnezzar, Constantine, Mohammed, the Inquisition and assimilation; they will know how to survive the motorcar.

But you—will you feel yourself a Jew, my child? People say to me " You are a Jew, because you were born a Jew; you neither willed it nor can change it." Will this explanation satisfy you if, though born a Jew, you no longer feel one?

When I was twenty I too felt I had no lot nor part in Israel; I was persuaded that Israel would disappear, and that in twenty years' time people would no longer speak of her. The twenty years have passed, and another twelve, and I have become a Jew again—so obviously, that I am asked " Why are you a Jew? "

What has happened to me can happen to you, my child. If you believe that the flame of Israel is extinguished in you, watch and wait: one day, it will burn again. This is a very old story, repeated in every generation: a thousand times Israel, it has seemed, must die, and a thousand times she has lived again. I want to tell you how she died and lived again in me, so that, if she dies in you, you in your turn can feel her born in you once more.

So I shall have brought Israel to you, and you shall bring her to others, if you will and can. And both of us, in our own way, will have preserved and handed on the divine commandment :

" Therefore shall ye lay up these my words in your heart and in your soul ; and ye shall bind them for a sign upon your hand, and they shall be for frontlets between your eyes. And ye shall teach them your children . . ."

ISRAEL LOST

I

When I was a little child I saw things which, by my fault, you will certainly never see. My father was a just man according to the Scriptures, and my mother was a smiling priestess at his hearth. Religion was, at that time, mingled with all the acts of their life, but so simply that I did not see it as religion.

It seemed natural that my father should, in the morning, wrap himself in a shawl of white wool with black stripes, and should bind lengths of leather on his forehead and left arm, while he murmured words which were not words. I thought grace after a meal as necessary as the meal itself ; and I felt no surprise when, on Friday evening, my mother stretched forth her fingers over the Sabbath candles, which shone through them and made them transparent.

Everything in the realm of food was governed by laws of hierarchy. One could not eat butter after meat, nor cut a chicken with a cheese knife : for there were two sets of utensils, one for meat and one for milk, and not to keep them distinct was a crime.

When a goose arrived from Strasbourg, on its neck would be a red seal with doubtful markings. These excited archaeological disputes in the kitchen; for my mother and Lisette, the cook, had to make sure, by a correct reading, at what hour of what day the bird had been killed, and whether therefore they were still permitted to make it into *confits*.

Ham, oysters, crayfish, game had only a nominal existence ; I had no idea of the taste, colour, or shape of these forbidden foods.

On Saturday, to ride in a tram would have seemed as wild an adventure as to ride to the moon, and to blow out a candle as mad as to blow out the sun.

Certain rites—but what a ceremonious word for such familiar things !—came round every year, as normally as the seasons that brought them. There was the palm branch to be waved, with its sweet citron ; and then there were the candles arranged on a board in a diminishing row, and we had to light them, beginning with the smallest and ending with the biggest.

Once a year I used to eat alone at midday; and when my brothers, who were old enough to fast, came back from synagogue, I admired the proud look on their drawn faces.

At another season my mother, with old Lisette, used to search for crumbs of leaven in every corner of the house and in every pocket of our clothes. Bread vanished from the table ; unleavened cakes took its place. At dinner my father, hat on head, sang Hebrew songs : the mortar and the bitter herbs passed from hand to hand : we drank four cups of wine, and opened the door, though there was no one to come in.

I did not know what all this meant ; I asked neither myself nor others. I only felt one thing : that on these occasions my parents' faces had a radiance of joy and serenity such as I have never seen since in the portraits of the greatest saints.

But it was not only impure food that was forbidden ; so were lying, laziness, greed, vulgarity, malice, and every kind of evil ; and if we were ruled by the familiar ceremonial of the home, no less clearly in command was the spirit of unity, of goodness, and of love.

This morality was not discussed : it was hardly even put into words. It was practised : like the daily ritual, it was life. Between my parents I never surprised a word that was not kind and courteous. To speak ill in their presence, to use an offensive or quarrelsome expression, would have been unthinkable. A gentle but strict justice punished our faults and rewarded our efforts to be good. The practice of thrift and hard work was an example to us in our every hour. Pleasure had its place, but was not an end in itself. Charity was exercised as a natural function. We consulted my father and submitted our disputes to him ; he gave out such an atmosphere of peace that the adversaries went away reconciled.

And these perfect manners, this ordered distinction of heart and mind, gave to what was a very humble home, reached by a dark stairway, all its light.

There was God, too : we lived with him, but his presence was implied ; we never talked of him. I did not hear his name, and spoke it only at the evening prayer which my mother, or Lisette, made me say before tucking me into bed. It was very short, this prayer : a few Hebrew words, which I repeated without understanding them, and then a single sentence : " God protect father and mother and everyone I love." But short though it was, it was this prayer which began to destroy my respect for our home observances.

After the light had been put out, I remained alone with this God to whom I had just said my lesson. Then I used to speak to him. How ? In what language ? How can I repeat it to you, my little unborn grandson ?

If you know in your turn that reaching towards the invisible ; if you experience, as I experienced, that contact with eternity ; if you silently pronounce that inner call : then you again will find the words which I found to serve me.

God was there, I knew well, very far and very near, everywhere and in my heart. I told him my faults and asked his pardon. I wished to be better, I could not be better without him. I promised him to do better, I begged him to help me. And he helped me, I was sure of it. I went up to him. He encompassed me, he took me ; I went to sleep in his arms.

Who had taught me to pray thus ? No one. But what value could there be in incomprehensible litanies and unexplained gestures, compared with this prayer that was without form or voice ? The words I am going to write will give a definiteness which was then lacking to my groping thought ; but I began to feel a contrast between my private prayer, which was very close to me, and my father's prayer, which I could not grasp. Or rather, only mine seemed a prayer ; the other was a habit, which God no longer noticed.

My critical sense was also stirring. On Saturdays, at school, I did no writing ; that was forbidden. But at college my brothers, who were older than I, wrote on Saturdays just as on week-days ; their studies required it. My father went to his office after synagogue on Saturdays and he also wrote ; his business required it. So it seemed, then, that the Sabbath rest was a serious matter only for the very young ?

Once I was taken on a journey. At the hotel butter and meat were all mixed up, cheese was served after the joint, and even ham appeared on the table. My parents broke, and let me break, the dietary laws. Food forbidden at home was, then, no longer forbidden outside the home ? The Law was no longer the Law ?

So, like every child in every age, I learned, in spite of myself, to watch my parents, and, drawing the logical conclusion from their lack of logic, to break, in all gentleness, their idols.

Others, without knowing it, abetted me. There was first of all my religion master, the synagogue cantor. He had a beautiful voice, a beautiful beard, and a beautiful soul. But, as a professor, he astonished me. I was going to college now, and was proud of my Latin. Now this man taught that Hebrew *had no grammar*—which made me doubtful both of the language and of its teacher. Then his method would of itself have discouraged the least curious intelligence: I had to stammer out a number of prayers, which he declared to be *untranslatable*. The catechism began with a phrase which amused me : " Who are you, my child ? I am a young Jewish *boy or girl*." And our sacred history, as chanted by my illiterate cantor — how poor it sounded after my Greek or Roman history !

My father, who used to read Hebrew at night, would say to me from time to time "It's so beautiful !". I didn't believe it. How should I have believed it ? My mind was out of harmony with Jewish values : nothing counted but the things I learned at school.

What had started with the cantor's ignorance was continued by the rabbi's irony. He sometimes came in to see us after dinner. We went back to our places at the table, poured him out a glass of Bordeaux, and listened.

With his side whiskers and clean-shaven lip, he was a fascinating talker. His wit delighted the whole town. Could I guess that his scepticism was a cover for his faith, and that his nature found its real happiness in proclaiming the divine unity ? Compared with the God who spoke to me at night, the caustic jests of his human representative seemed to me all too human.

From the eminence of his Chair in Comparative Philology at the University, he scoffed at the small tradesmen of his community, which nevertheless he served with all his heart. If you were to believe him, the Jewish tailor would reach out from his shop as he passed by and finger the stuff of his rabbinical coat-tails, because he bought his clothes from the Christian tailor ; and the cattle dealer on the look out for a good match for his daughter would say " I don't sell cattle, I manufacture them." Then there were the Jewish stories, those excellent Jewish stories that made me laugh but also blush a little : the two Jewish diners who leave the door of a restaurant open as they go out on a stormy night, and mutter, when they are abused for doing it, " There you are — antisemites ! " : or Moses playing écarté with God in paradise, and saying " Now, Lord, no miracles ! "

This gallery of portraits and this collection of stories, amusing though they were, disfigured Israel still more for my too sensitive soul. And I could not forget these grotesque pictures when I went, reluctantly enough in any case, to synagogue.

In accordance with custom, I had first been taken there when a very small boy to roll round one of the sacred scrolls a long band of cloth, covered with coloured letters. I was wearing my velvet suit with the mother-of-pearl buttons, and was in the seventh heaven of delight. My mother looked down on me from the gallery, and the stars of gold painted on the vault seemed to me real stars in a real sky.

But now I knew the cantor and the rabbi too well ; and they robbed the place of its fascination. Except in rare moments which the music made radiant, or when the secret splendour of the ceremonial shone out suddenly in its manifest beauty, what weariness I felt during those heavy hours, which were made still heavier by the endless repetition of

phrases in an unknown language ; what physical irritation
at these mannerless people who read their newspapers or
talked aloud ; and what disgust when I heard the only words
that were spoken in French, for to stimulate generosity
they announced, under the very eye of the Sacred Law
the exact amount of each offering !

And when, at the age of thirteen, I made what a Christian would call my first communion, in the morning, facing
the Ark, I could chant in perfect tune the biblical text, no
word of which I understood ; and in the evening, after the
banquet, I could recite in a single breath the benediction
which was still Hebrew to me ; but at night, when I was
alone in my bed, face to face with the God who visited me, I
asked myself confusedly if he was really the God of Israel.

He was, my child. All these prayers, of which the sense
escaped me, revealed him magnificently ; all these rites,
which made me so lonely by their seeming emptiness, were
his sacraments. But I did not know this, for I had been
badly taught ; and I had to wander a long time among men
and thoughts before I reached this truth.

What a strange way to explain, you will say, why I am
a Jew. But you will only understand why I am a Jew if you
first understand why I had ceased to be one.

In these gentle days of my adolescence, the rupture was
not yet apparent. It was simply that my spirit, without
knowing it, was turning away from the spirit of my people.
But now I was going to discover another world.

II

I had overworked a little in my fourteenth year. My
great friend of those days, a class-mate, now a pastor and
professor of theology, lived in the country. I needed pure air ;
his mother was very ready to welcome me. I played the
piano ; and a neighbour, for love of music, invited me to her
home, where I became a daily guest.

She was an old lady, living there with her daughter and
three sons, two of whom were already men. Widow of a cele-
brated writer, she had known " Monsieur Taine," " Mon-

sieur Renan " and " Monsieur Got," and had travelled for
many years in Italy. Her talk was full of memories. At home,
we respected intellectual culture ; here, one lived familiarly
with it.

The house, a very simple one, looked out over a great
meadow ; and this in its turn commanded the cliff at a point
where the Rhône, with widened stream, twists round in a
rocky amphitheatre. My old friend taught me to see nature
for the first time. The play of clouds and the dramas of light
were events for her, and so they became for me.

I could not quite make out just what it was that appeared new to me in this home ; but a harmony ruled there
altogether different from the harmony that I had
known. Strange and tiresome as already seemed to me the
religious observances which gave rhythm, for us Jews, to
days and months and years, I had never imagined the possi-
bility of existence without them. And now here were
no dietary laws, no imperative rites, no burdensome pro-
hibitions. One went to church on Sunday, that was all. Or
rather, it was not all. At home, work, charity and goodness
were just practised, but here we had a clear consciousness of
living them : and the moral instinct was lit up and enriched
by all the radiance that living speech can give it.

Then this mother, these brothers, this sister, were so free
of one another in their decided preferences ! Whether it was
a question of a walk, of something to praise or blame, or of
a decision, even a serious one, to take or set aside, each of
them expressed a taste just as if it were proper to have
tastes in isolation. The ancestral spirit of community that
ruled at home would have prevented such divergences. And
I felt myself in obscure revolt against it.

I have since understood what was happening to me then.
At Geneva, where I was born, the clans remained quite
separate ; I had never really lived any life but the Jewish.
No chains shut in our ghetto ; but it was a ghetto none the
less. For the first time, I was leaving it. I was seeing the free
air and the free sky ; and my spirit was emancipating itself
not only from the rites of the Jewish family, but from the
Jewish family itself.

The following winter, a book separated me still further
from Israel : the Gospel. It was not my friends who were

responsible for this tremendous discovery ; their delicacy would not have permitted it. But I, whom no one had ever been able to interest in the Old Testament, wanted to know this Jesus who was preached to them on Sundays. I can still see, under the trees of the old square, the shop-window of the secondhand bookseller who sold me, for a few centimes, all the suffering of this revelation. I can still hear, in my breast, my heart's cry as I furtively read the immortal pages. I was the shepherd by the manger, I was the fisher of Tiberias : I walked with the paralytic, I saw again with the blind man, I returned to life with Lazarus : the " Our Father " was my prayer, the Sermon on the Mount my sermon, the agony on the Cross my agony. But, at the end of my Passion, I did not murmur, like Christ, "Father, for-give them, for they know not what they do." No : crucified with horror and shame for my race, I cried out, I remember, in the solitude of my room, so little as I was, " Dirty Jews, dirty Jews."

I have described poetically, in *L'Enfant Prophète*, my agony of those days. I do not wish to go over it again. But to show you that this story was not merely a story, and to make clear to you what I dared to call at that distant time " my religious thought," I want to copy out for you here, without touching up the clumsiness of the style, what I wrote then in the Diary which I found the other evening under some old papers :

" I am not a believer ; my old religion prevents it, my poor religion, the ruins of a building that was never finished. What concern for forms ! These absurd customs, these rules about not eating ham and not tearing paper on Saturday, this habit of eating unleavened bread for seven days, have long since revolted me, without my daring to face it. What in the end has freed me from all that is the reading of the New Testament. I have wept real tears over the torment of Jesus and I have felt shame for my ancestors who defiled themselves with the blood of this righteous man whom they so treacherously crucified. Yes, I have felt shame for my race. People say to me ' A Jew and a Christian can never agree.' But I am not a Jew. Perhaps it is shameful so to abandon in one's heart the faith of one's ancestors, but I cannot see that I am called upon to copy their mistakes. My

opinions are my own, no one has taught me them, they do
not come out of books. I am told that only Christians can
understand their religion, because their religion is the life of
Jesus. It is also mine, for that beautiful life is what I make
my example : that charity and mercy are what I admire :
that is what my soul loves, and finds truly great. I understand Jesus, but I do not think of him as a supernatural
being, for that would be beyond my intelligence, nor do I
shut my eyes and believe him divine, for that would be
beneath it. I even understand Jesus better than I could ever
understand a God who was the absolute master and judge
of the whole universe. It is not that I am an atheist, far from
it. I pray every night, but the God to whom I pray is within
me, and is not a master. They say ' God is a spirit.' Why
should he not be an idea that speaks in the conscience of
everyone ? I admire and envy whole-hearted faith, but alas !
I do not possess it. I cannot be a Jew. I cannot be a Christian.
But if I can follow him whom I take as my model, if I think
of goodness as God and believe that it is perhaps the
manifestation of a God Almighty, am I very blameworthy ?
May I be pardoned if I am wrong, and if I have doubted
may I in later years find mercy in Heaven ! Oh God, let
thy light shine in me, and if thou livest reveal thyself
unto me ! "

Since I wrote this I have revised my verdict on the trial
of Jesus : and I hope that you, my child, being better in-
formed, will never know the first grief of my life, the grief
of accusing our whole race.

But this God of my prayers, the most precious remnant,
and the only one, of my Jewish heritage : this God who, for
all the cold name of Goodness that I was already giving him,
dwelt in me with so living a presence that I still spoke to him
as I would to a friend, even this God was going to leave my
heart.

It happened the following year, and in the most commonplace fashion. I wanted to be a philosopher, and as there
was no philosophy class at Geneva I plunged without a guide
into the thousand pages of a book that promised adventure :
*Selected Texts . . . The Great Schools . . . The Leading
Systems* . . . At last I was going to know !

Quick ! I open the thick volume ! . . . Religion first !

. . . What, so many thoughts about God, and so contra
dictory ?

Not a word about the God of Israel : is he then of no
importance ? But I learn that a certain Protagoras would
leave undecided whether the gods exist or not, and that a
certain Critias considers that they were invented by a law
giver as prudent as he was cunning. Socrates, I am told
revealed the moral God, the God of "civilised nations.'
Plato placed him in the " world of Ideas." Aristotle identi
fied him with "pure activity": the Stoics drew no distinc
tion between his unity and the unity of the universe : and
Plotinus made a trinity of him ! What to believe ? Whom
to follow ? I was perplexed.

In the Middle Ages, the same disputes translated into
scholastic jargon : St. Augustin differs from St. Thomas
Aquinas, Averrhoes disagrees with Scotus Erigena ! . .
In modern times the fight goes on : Malebranche against
Descartes ! Leibniz against Spinoza !

There were of course the proofs, those famous proofs o
the existence of God. But I had read too much : the
proofs proved nothing to me. What triumph I felt when Kant
arrived with his great club, and knocked into dust all these
confident assertions ! Ah ! how well he spoke, how right he
was ! Yes, we impose on things the laws of our own thinking
we cannot conceive them in themselves ; we know neither
Being, nor Substance, nor the Absolute, nor God.

Then, like a conjurer, Herbert Spencer came on the
scene, holding in his hands the theory of evolution. Thrice
he shot out his cuffs, and I saw the One producing the Many
and the Simple making the Complex, from the humblest
atom to the highest creations of the intellect. Two passes
and, magically, Vegetable emerged from Mineral, and Man
from Animal! A flick of the finger: and from Heredity and the
Association of Ideas came tumbling out those old illusions
Good, Evil, Liberty and God !

But it was Auguste Comte and his positivism which at
last made everything quite clear to me. Humanity, it was
obvious, had passed through three stages. In the theological
period, men explained natural phenomena by supernatural
causes, marvels, miracles, acts of God ; in the metaphysical
period, they had recourse to materialised abstractions,

faculties, essence, accident ; in the third period, which is still with us, we happily confine ourselves to understanding, by observation and experiment, the interconnection of phenomena. This last method, which alone is valid, has created modern science and takes the place for ever of metaphysics and theology ; the only religion now is the Religion of Humanity ; the matter is settled.

At this discovery of the great void, the foundations of my inner life were deeply undermined. I ought to have collapsed : but nothing of the kind happened.

I was too proud of being a philosopher and of pitying the errors that surrounded me. My conversations with my God of the night changed their tone : a little while ago, I had cried again and again in my anguish " If thou livest, reveal thyself unto me " : now the words were no longer a prayer, but a summons. I defied this God, I blasphemed against him. Then I gave up the attempt to draw speech from what doesn't exist, and left him to his silence.

Great as was the gulf which separated me at that time from Israel, I was about to widen it. I came to Paris, I passed my *rhétorique supérieure*, I attended the Sorbonne, I entered the *Ecole normale*. All this ought to have made me reasonable ; it had the opposite effect. I should like to mingle, with some severity for what I then was, a good deal of indulgent irony ; but I must confess that as I approached my twentieth year I reached a height of pretentiousness from which later on, in view of evidence that came my way, I had unhappily to descend. Pretending to succumb to what I was happy to call *my* charm, some of my friends amused themselves by forming round me a little court, which tempered loyalty with chaff. People called us " the aesthetes " and I rather feel that they were right.

I had chosen for my special attention Anatole France and Renan, and it was water drawn at the pure source of these masters that I adulterated with my dilettantism. For dilettanti we were !

One must not take the world seriously ; one did not know whether it existed, for one left coarse certainties to the vulgar. Society was not worth the trouble of mixing with it ; of what importance to subtle minds were " eternal truths," or " the rights of man and the citizen," or party strife, or the constitution of States ? Ethics, too, seemed a very heavy affair: good and evil were dumb-bells that one didn't handle.

Only art counted, not merely the art of words, of sounds, of shapes, and of colours, which was after all available to the inferior bipeds who could read a book or listen to a concert or visit a museum—but the art of composing, out of the successive phases of one's own experience, a work that would be worthy of contemplation.

My chief function, then, was to admire myself ; and as, amid the shifting sands that were the moments of my life, it would have seemed poor to admire in myself one person only, I distinguished at least five, each of whom corresponded to one of my friends. There was the Des Grieux bored by a Tiberge, the Pylades whose Orestes was always bitter, the Agathon of a modern Socrates, and then the ironist who juggled with the shadow of things, and the romantic whose piano suffered now ecstasy and now madness.

Could a being so complex inhabit this vile world without peril ? What if life, by compelling him to be more simple, should rob him of his dignity ? It was decided to forestall such a disaster. My Socrates, for whom one hemlock episode more or less could hold no terror, brought me a phial of poison . . . and, if he had not taken care to fill it with pure water, you would never have had a grandfather !

Do not think, my child, that I revive the past simply for the satisfaction of making a show with my memories. If there is a quality—or a defect—that is commonly attributed to Israel, it is, surely, concern for this earthly existence. Idealist or materialist, the Jew clings to life, whether to exploit it or ennoble it. To turn away from it, to abdicate before the due hour, in contemplation, in inaction, or in death, is not the act of a Jew. I had abandoned the rites and statutes of my family. I had rejected their God. And now the deepest voice of my race was silent within me.

ISRAEL FOUND AGAIN

I

That was where I stood when it was first mooted that Captain Alfred Dreyfus, banished as a traitor to Devil's Island in 1894, had been unjustly condemned, simply because he was a Jew. At first the whole thing seemed to me quite uninteresting ; it was newspaper scribble, powerless to disturb my contemplation. If I had consented to give it the least attention, I should have thought it improbable ; absurd to imagine that seven officers should send an innocent man to prison simply from prejudice.

But the agitation on behalf of the condemned man was growing throughout the country ; several of our teachers were interested in his case ; he soon had supporters among my friends at the *Ecole*, even among the aesthetes ; and detached as I was from the contingencies of this earth, for Dreyfus even I had to come down from my heaven.

I had a great friend who was not at the *Ecole* with me. We had got to know one another at college, and were soon united by ties of affection which still endure. Our deep tenderness was assuming the appearance of a wholly intellectual inter-course. It was our joy to understand one another, and to bring our ideas into harmony. I experienced, it seemed to me, a certain pride in preserving this aspect of our friendship. I was anxious that the substance of it should be neither the mutual service which I thought of as the current coin of sentiment, nor even that commonplace trust which shows itself in the exchange of secrets. But the fact was that, close though our two souls were, a certain uneasiness separated them. The Dreyfus Affaire was to show me why.

Brought up in a *milieu* to which anything reactionary or even conservative was foreign, very sensitive, but with a sensitiveness devoid of romanticism, steeped in the subversive nonchalance of which Maurice Barrès was the exponent in his first period, wonderfully intelligent, and far more steadfast than I in obedience to logic (we will call him, if you like, the Logician), he had taken our common nihilism to its logical conclusion. Honest and free in mind as he was, he had emancipated himself from all philosophical illusions and had broken all the social idols ; his critical sense rejected even the idea of a country to which some special loyalty might be due.

His all-embracing scepticism at first admitted, unlike mine, that Dreyfus might well be innocent ; but the nearer I was brought to this view of the matter as revelation succeeded revelation, the more, to my great surprise, I saw my friend's judgment developing in the opposite direction.

Before long it was stated that in violation of the rights of the defence a secret dossier had been submitted to Dreyfus' military judges and had perhaps decided their verdict, without the accused or his Counsel having ever been in a position to discuss it. This seemed to me to create a presumption in the Captain's favour : what need of secret proofs, if the others were sufficient ? For my Logician, this reasoning was valid only in the realm of pure abstraction : one couldn't tell, he said, whether it was applicable to the actual facts.

The violation of legality, which shocked me profoundly, was in itself sufficient, I thought, to justify a retrial. No, he replied, it might derive from interests higher than those of the defence, and to compel a retrial the reasons adduced must be more peremptory.

It was known that Dreyfus had been condemned on the evidence of a note written, so it was claimed, in his handwriting, and listing the documents delivered to a foreign Power. Now when this note was published in the press the writing was seen to bear a strange resemblance to that of another officer, Major Esterhazy : indeed, a great number of experts declared that they were identical. " What do they know about it ? " answered the Logician. " They have only been working on facsimiles."

In my opinion the motives that would have explained Dreyfus' crime had never been clearly disentangled ; Esterhazy, on the other hand, was ruined, and he was known to have written letters in which he expressed the lesire that France should suffer another Sedan. Esterhazy, replied my friend, may be a scoundrel, without Dreyfus' being any the less guilty. Then these letters of which people talk—are they authentic?

If Colonel Picquart was accused of forgery in his attempts to prove that the General Staff was covering Esterhazy, my Logician saw nothing improbable in the charge; but if it was established that Major Henry had committed forgery to stop the retrial, this forgery became the patriotic act of a devoted soldier who, with his knowledge of documents which could not be produced without danger, had had no motive other than that of supplying substitutes.

What struck me in all this reasoning was that it was irrefutable provided only that one admitted the implied premiss, which was nothing but a tacit vote of confidence in the military tribunal and the General Staff. But there was nothing superstitious in my friend's confidence; it was, he said, confidence in the only men who had the necessary information. He saw, on the one hand, specialists who *knew*; on the other, amateurs who *supposed*; and in choosing between the two he did not hesitate.

I did, at first, and for a considerable time; then I hesitated no longer. And now the people my Logician called amateurs, those who in his opinion supposed, in my opinion knew. With each new incident (and there was a new incident every day) we argued and tried to convince one another. We did not succeed. I was worried. I could not doubt his intelligence, or his good faith, or his heart. What was the clash that made him see error where I saw truth? His confidence in certain officers ought to have been a mere provisional finding of his critical faculty; but didn't something else insinuate itself into this confidence without his knowing it, something instinctive and more obscure? And in my own case, if I felt confidence in others could I say quite certainly that there was nothing in me that came between my judgment and the facts? What were these unconscious forces that made us oppose one another? Why did I fear them without defining them? Were they going to destroy our beautiful friendship?

It was reasonable to fear that they might, for all around us old ties were being weakened. You will perhaps read in

your history book an account of the Affaire ; but what you
will miss is the stridency of the passions which it rendered
vocal. Lectures at the Sorbonne would develop into meet-
ings, and evening parties into free fights. Guards were often
on the streets ; long lines of police, or even of troops, held
back the crowd, which howled down, turn by turn, scoun-
drels and heroes. This civil strife destroyed the domestic
happiness, and even the peace itself, of the simplest homes.
Whether one was for Dreyfus or against him, one was always
the enemy of someone : a friend, it might be, of fifty years'
standing, or even a brother or father. For behind the drama
of the Affaire there loomed, nameless and vast, another
drama, which brought together in the clash of hatred two
ideas of society, of life, and of the world.

The clearest aspect of this hidden conflict was the struggle centering round Israel. Dreyfus being a Jew, certain
antidreyfusards held all Jews responsible for his crime, and
for the disturbances caused throughout the country by their
furious determination to exonerate him. Even given his innocence as proved, the Jews would still be guilty of wishing
to save him : the honour of a Jew was not to be compared
with the safety of a nation. If thinkers with no religious ties,
or Christians, or Catholics, or even priests (there were a number of them) were to be found among his supporters, that
was because they had been corrupted by Jewish gold or the
Jewish spirit. A great syndicate had been formed, they said,
the Syndicate of Treason, with a treasury fed by Jewish for-
tunes from all over the world ; and it was in the service of
men who were plotting to disarm France so as to betray her
to her enemies. After all, there was nothing new in this.
Wherever the Jew passed he brought ruin. He had undermined the Roman Empire and made common cause with the
Barbarians at the time of the great irruptions. It was by his
fault that Spain of the Visigoths surrendered to the Arabs
and that Poland of Poniatowski was partitioned. After ex-
torting all the world's gold by usury in the Middle Ages, he
used it to finance for his own convenience the Revolution
of 1789 : which, by disguising him everywhere as a citizen,
enabled him to follow, down the whole length of a debased
century, and on the polluted ruins of a vanished order, his
dream of dissolute power. Greedy, sensual, a forger and a

chief, the Jew was, then, a traitor by nature and by choice ; and if, in Dreyfus' case, one must find a motive for his crime, the mere fact that he was a Jew explained his treason.

This philosophy of history by the method of abuse should not have troubled me. Digging down into the most secret recesses of my subconscious, I failed to recognise myself in this portrait of a Jew, and I knew very well that I was hatching no sinister plot which might cause the world uneasiness. But while I did not feel personally involved, I became irritable. This antisemitism was something new to me.

When quite little I had, of course, heard of the pogroms in Russia which had followed a Tsar's assassination. Women disembowelled, old men buried alive, infants soaked in petrol and then thrown on to the flames—these pictures had haunted my nights, but they had faded.

I had also often listened to talk about *richès*. This word, from the Yiddish of Alsace, meant the ill-will of Christians towards Jews. But I had felt bound to take note, on more than one occasion, that effects quite easy to explain by other causes were readily attributed to this sentiment ; and for that reason I had always found something symbolic in the story of the two Jewish diners and the draught, which our rabbi told so maliciously.

My mother, French by birth, had often said to me that in France Jews were happier than anywhere else, and that we must take to our hearts the generous people who had been the first to grant us the rights of citizenship and had honoured a Jewish minister, Crémieux, with a national funeral.

A great stir had been made since then by a book entitled *La France Juive*, which in violent language attributed to Israel all the country's misfortunes ; but that, I was told, was a mere piece of literary invective, and it had never occurred to me to attach any importance to it.

After my arrival in Paris certain papers had, on the occasion of the scandalous Panama affair and then of the first Dreyfus trial, returned to these charges and made them the basis of a campaign. But was I reading the papers at that time ? I was living deep in a country to which no voice penetrated from without ; such vulgarities seemed to me unworthy of an attention occupied with transcendental visions.

Besides, why should I have given heed to the enemies of Israel ? Was I heeding Israel herself ? Did anybody about me feel concern for her? Did my friends at the *Ecole* see any difference between them and me ? For them, as for me, the Jew had disappeared.

Even in my family, so attached to the old observances, they were going, these observances, one by one. Peacefully, without any fuss or discussion, by the simple pressure of surrounding forces, the rules, but recently so rigid, were being modified year after year by new exceptions. When I returned to Geneva for the holidays, I would note on each occasion some progress in this work of disintegration : the festivals were less strictly observed, the rites were less constantly repeated : even ham appeared on the menu, and to the great scandal of Lisette, the Catholic cook who in the old days had made me say my Hebrew prayer and who was alone now in preserving unimpaired her respect for the regulations, butter and meat followed one another in the wrong order and the two sets of utensils were mixed into one.

Since at this patriarchal hearth Israel was already so sick, she was clearly going to die everywhere, as she had died in me ; all that remained was to let her die.

Then why this irritation in me against antisemitism, this irritation that grew every day ? What had I in common with the people they attacked ? What did it matter to me whether the attacks were justified or not ?

At any rate, I thought, this pain I felt would soon vanish ? Or was I really going to waste my time over the insults of pamphleteers who were devoid of all critical sense? I might well have calmed myself and let it go with a shrug of the shoulders, if my Logician had not had in store for me, on this point, a new surprise ; for he stated that, without agreeing with the form of these polemics, he was less sure than I of their inanity. There was certainly no lack of subtlety in his thinking ; but that proved its sincerity, and obliged me to reflect.

"The word antisemitism " he said "is a label for a number of very different aspirations. There is the antisemitism that derives solely from the Catholic faith as such : this is the most negligible sort, and if you wish to find the most determined of antisemites on purely religious grounds, you must perhaps still go to the Protestants. The most popular variety simply aims at robbing those in possession; a few fools and knaves, blindly assisted by men whose honesty outruns their intelligence, have contrived to persuade the mob that all its misfortunes come from the Jews, and that any attack on them is legitimate, even to the point of pillage and massacre."

" At the same time," he added, " one mustn't forget the feelings of a people that sees itself more or less completely governed by a tiny minority, and by a race which it has had the habit (why ? that doesn't matter today) of despising for so many centuries."

That Israel has her idealists, her dreamers and her mystics, indifferent to the narrower interests of Jewry, this he recognised ; but he saw in these sublime spirits nothing but politicians of disaster, for they built in the realm of fantasy, while we lived in the world of fact.

That certain Israelites, more intelligent than the generality of men, can give, in the real world, more than their due of service—that they can even, on occasion, show themselves better patriots, he did not deny. But too many Jews, in his opinion, held too many offices, for the first crisis revealed, in the persistence of their solidarity, their lack of national sense.

Wishing then to feel confidence in those whom one entrusted with the administration of one's country, and to see reflected in them that country's interests and sentiments, my dear Logician could see nothing illogical in the idea, not indeed of excluding Jews absolutely from public life, but of restricting their influence proportionately to their relative numbers.

I was astounded. Were the Jews then really governing France ? Must they be deprived of the rights that they had fought for and won ? Was it from solidarity that they believed Dreyfus innocent ?

How could a clear and passionless intelligence accept or even conceive such enormities ? I sought for an answer in vain, and I could not distract my mind from the attempt to find one.

It was a sad evening when I suddenly realised that between my friend and myself agreement was impossible, and that our lack of it had its real source neither in the facts, nor in their interpretation, nor in the more or less sharp ideas which we were basing on them, but in a reality with deeper roots in ourselves, and more real than our selves, which eluded us. I was now closely engaged in the Dreyfus struggle, and had signed a protest in the papers in favour of Picquart. My friend, with an affectionate delicacy characteristic of him, had conveyed to me that, as a foreigner or half-foreigner, I ought to have abstained from this public declaration. In sound logic he was right ; but I tried, in a letter, to persuade him of the contrary.

" Admit for a moment " I wrote " that all who signed had excellent reasons for doing so, and that their reasons are my reasons. Did I, by signing, arrogate to myself a right that I did not possess ? Am I violating any French law by giving my opinion, by expressing my personal feelings, my pain and my indignation ? This is not a political matter but a judicial one. I find an abuse of power, an act of tyranny covered by a pretence of enforcing the law; foreigners living in France are as liable to suffer from it as Frenchmen. They have only to leave the country, you will say ? Yes, if it were the actual laws of the country that displeased them : but they may stay and protest, when faced with a breach of the law which dismays numerous Frenchmen no less than themselves.

" Given the right to protest," I added, " I saw it as a duty to do so, for I felt bound to express publicly a point of view that I had not concealed from my friends. The intentions of the Minister, who disliked the *Ecole*, were well known ; and if disciplinary measures had been taken against the signatories it would have been painful for me to be spared."

That is how I reasoned after the event ; but my signature had not been prompted by reasoning. I was becoming a social creature ; for the first time I was acting ; and I was finding that action results not only from clear reasoning, capable of intellectual exposition, but from an impulse as strong as its origin is obscure. I felt that my dilettantism had

een nothing more than a façade, that justice was a
ecessity for me, that those humanitarian illusions at
vhich I had mocked were my own, and that reality would
ever disillusion me to the point of making me doubt
he truth of certain old ideas which were childlike and
enerous, mouthed though they might be by a number
f idiots.

Did there mingle with this human solidarity a Jewish
olidarity, which made more painful for me the drama I was
iving ? I could no longer doubt it, I was certain of it. But
vhat of that ? I could resist the appeal neither of the one
or of the other ; both were imperatives for me, part of
ny very nature.

And I saw my friend so different, so distant ! Had we
een in harmony with one another for so long merely
ecause I had been, for just so long, ignorant of myself ?
he uneasiness I had felt so often in his presence, did it
ark a gulf that nothing now could ever bridge ? Must
ve give up what we had in common ? Delicate though it
vas, did not his friendly reproach banish me at once from
is country and from his friendship ?

And while I was considering these sad questions, the
ffaire was becoming for me a personal ordeal. How far
way already was my transcendant egoism ! I waited for the
apers with anguish. I read them as if the fate of this man
vas bound up with my own fate and with the fate of his
vhole race, in which, little by little, I was rediscovering my
wn. His letters had been published. Under the clumsiness of
he declamatory style I heard the cry of tortured innocence.
nd, coming to me across the seas, this cry trembled in my
hroat and tore my heart. At night, in my bed, I thought of
he prisoner : I saw him, alone on his tropical rock with the
alignant silence of his gaolers. He also was lying
nder the night, pinioned to his mattress of straw by
wo rings of iron. And, motionless, he cried, he cried. And
is cry reawakened other cries, those of the distant po-
rom which I had been told of in my childhood. They
ecame present to me again, those vanished images : the
isembowelled women, the old men buried alive, the children
hrown naked on to the flames. And I wished to rise from my

bed and cry out in my turn, to cry their martyrdom to a
the world.

And when, brought back from his island by his judges
Dreyfus was, at Rennes, condemned for the second time, m
life stopped. I could not eat, I felt myself banished from th
brotherhood of men. And I asked myself : " Jew, what i
your place in the world ? "

II

My friendship with my dear Logician had come throug
this agony. His tact proved stronger than my nervous sensi
bility. Why should we quarrel, he said, because we don'
agree ? Can't we try to understand one another, withou
trying to make our two persons one ? Our conversations wil
no longer be dialogues, but monologues that intersect
each of us will speak his thoughts without wishing to con
vert the other. Perhaps that will be a better way of bein
in harmony ? There have been examples of such a friendship

And in fact all uneasiness ceased ; conscious of ou
differences, we came to be friends who could say any
thing to one another. And, in the joy of a new affection
he confided to me his new ideas, which gave me my bear
ings in the chaos of my own.

He had now descended, like me, from the serene space
in which our dilettantism had delighted ; and had come t
the point of believing that, if knowledge is vain, even vaine
is the eternal repetition of this axiom, and that, if we canno
achieve any certitude about the meaning of life or abou
morality, it is more profitable to choose a definite direction
even an arbitrary one, than to be for ever entrusting onesel
to the caprices, whether more or less rational, of one'
own sensibility. He aspired to social life, and was preparin
to accept its demands. Now on what could an intelligence s
logical as his base its activity ? A stranger to the revolu
tionary tradition, as to every other, he had been unable t
accept as proven truth the gospel of the Rights of Mar
which, proclaimed by the Revolution, was the source of al
the political philosophy on which modern society rests
Following the critique of Comte, Taine, Renan, and Barrès

he could see in this philosophy nothing but mystical out-pourings towards vague entities, nothing but reasonings, more or less vicious, from improbable hypotheses, nothing but a pity that was either sterile or the begetter of hatred. And what precisely irritated him in the Affaire was that the Dreyfusards drew from this revolutionary gospel, which they claimed to be unquestionable, the very substance of their questionable intervention. Humanitarianism, in a word, seemed to him to demand an act of faith that was not necessarily more reasonable than any other.

What, then, was left to him of certainty ? Nothing, except that indefinable heritage from the past stored up in tastes and nerves and sensibility, that *je ne sais quoi* which makes a Frenchman feel closer to a Frenchman than to a German or even to a Belgian or Swiss. Unable to rest on any principle, he went back to a tradition, to the tradition nearest to him, to that whose maxims were the least opposed to his own nature, to that of which he himself was the result, and which he preferred just because it was his. In a word he adopted with all his heart the concept of fatherland which he had criticised previously as narrow and vulgar, but which now seemed to him fuller and more real than that of humanity. Granted all this, it was simply a question of building the future greatness of France by drawing correct conclusions from the facts of her history : one must apply to the circumstances of today the rules of action that had raised her high in the past.

Rediscovering in this way a whole world buried deep within him, my friend, in his great kindness, pressed me to make a similar study of the traditions I had inherited from my race, as a means of recovering the inner peace that was leaving me. Everything disposed me to follow his advice : since the beginning of the Dreyfus affair the Jewish question had seemed to me a reality, now it appeared tragic:

" What is Judaism ?—A danger, they say, for the society to which you belong. What danger ? . . But first, am I still a Jew ? I have abandoned the Jewish religion. . . You are a Jew all the same. How ? Why ? What ought I to do ? Must I kill myself because I am a Jew ? "

At moments, I envied the strong and narrow faith of my ancestors. Penned in their ghettos by contempt and hatred,

they at least knew why. But I knew nothing. How could
learn ?

Of Israel I was entirely ignorant. And I regretted all th
years I had spent in the study of philosophy, of Germani
philology and of comparative literature. I ought to hav
learned Hebrew, to have studied my race, its origins, it
beliefs, its rôle in history, its place among the huma:
groups today ; I ought to have attached myself, through m
race, to something that would be myself and more tha
myself, and to have continued, through her, something tha
others had begun and that others after me would continue

And I told myself that if I made some other use of m
life, if I devoted myself to some other study, if later
founded a family without being able to bequeath to m
children some ancestral ideal, I should always experience a:
obscure remorse, the vague feeling of having failed in
duty. And I remembered my dead father, I reproache
myself with not having understood that Jewish wisdom c
which he talked to me and which lived in him—and with n
longer finding, by my own fault, anything in commo
between Israel's past and my own empty soul.

It was then that, for the first time, I heard of Zionism
You cannot imagine what a light that was, my child
Remember that, at the period of which I am writing, th
word Zionism had never yet been spoken in my presenc
The antisemites accused the Jews of forming a nation withi
the nations ; but the Jews, or at any rate those whom I cam
across, denied it. And now here were the Jews declarin
" We are a people like other peoples ; we have a country jus
as the others have. Give us back our country."

I made enquiries : the Zionist idea, it appeared, had it
origins far back in the days of the ancient prophets ; th
Bible promised the Jews of the Dispersion that they shoul
return to the Holy Land ; during the whole of the Midd]
Ages, only their faith in this promise kept them alive ; in th
eighteenth and nineteenth centuries, such great spirits a
Maurice de Saxe, the Prince de Ligne and Napoleon ha
caught a glimpse of the philanthropic, political, economi
religious and moral advantages which a resettlement of th
Jews in Palestine might offer ; since 1873 colonies had bee

founded there and were developing ; and now a new apostle, Theodor Herzl, was calling upon the Jews of the whole world to found the Jewish State.

Was this the solution for which I was looking ? It explained so many things. If the Jews really formed but a single nation, one began to understand why they were considered Jews even when they ceased to practise their religion, and it became credible, too, that a nation which had welcomed them should be able to accuse them of not always being devoted to its national interests. Then the Zionist idea moved me by its sublimity ; I admired in these Jews, and would have wished to be able to admire in myself, this fidelity to the ancestral soil which still lived after two thousand years, and I trembled with emotion as I pictured the universal exodus which would bring them home, from their many exiles, to the unity that they had reconquered.

My Logician, for his part, applauded my growing enthusiasm. He saw clearly that the Zionism to which I might be coming not only harmonised well with his new-born nationalism, but even accepted some of its antisemitic conclusions; in this way our two minds would have followed two parallel roads, both deserting the concept of humanity for that of fatherland, and the fatherland being, for me, the Jewish fatherland. But from the beginning I had once more the confused feeling that my logic was less strict than his, and that, if I wished to follow my usual habit of being sincere with myself, I could not adopt, in all its severity, the whole of his reasoning.

The third Zionist Congress was about to open at Basle. I decided to attend it. My knowledge of German enabled me to follow the debates pretty closely. Theodor Herzl gave an account of his attempts to obtain a charter from the Sultan. The report of the Actions Committee showed that a hundred thousand Jews were already enrolled in the organisation, and drew the inference that at least half a million Jews throughout the world were already Zionists. The Congress rejected a plan for Jewish colonisation in Cyprus, which was brought forward in opposition to colonisation in Palestine. The argument of certain anti-zionists, who saw in the movement a danger to non-zionist Jews, was refuted.

So much ability, so much eloquence, so much faith! I listened to it all; but, with even greater interest, I looked about me. What Jewish contrasts! A pale-faced Pole with high cheek-bones, a German in spectacles, a Russian looking like an angel, a bearded Persian, a clean-shaven American, an Egyptian in a fez, and, over there, that black phantom, towering up in his immense caftan, with his fur cap and pale curls falling from his temples. And, in the presence of all these strange faces, the inevitable happened; I felt myself a Jew, very much a Jew, but also very French, a Frenchman of Geneva, but French none the less.

I now well understood that the Zionist programme in no way implies the return of all Jews to Palestine—a thing numerically impracticable: the Jewish fatherland is only for those Jews who feel they have no other. Now I was French on my mother's side, and my heart and mind had always gone out to France. At first, when I was quite small, there was the gratitude of my parents as Jews towards that country; then came my literary aspirations, then my long residence in Paris with fellow-students whose camaraderie and friendship had helped me to become what I was; and finally the Dreyfus drama, which was an agony for me in an agonised France. In my thoughts, I could not separate my little fatherland, Geneva, from that great spiritual fatherland to which even Geneva in so many ways belongs. When, therefore, I abandoned my dilettante egoism, and, like my dear Logician, tried to find deep down in me a tradition, I found, stronger and more conscious than the Jewish instincts, which were only just beginning to wake in me, the French tradition, mingled with that of Israel.

What then, for me, was Zionism? It could enthrall me it enthralls me still, this great miracle of Israel which concerns the whole of Israel: three million Jews will speak Hebrew, will live Hebrew on Hebrew soil! But, for the twelve million Jews who will remain scattered throughout the world, for them and for me, the tragic question remained: What is Judaism? What ought a Jew to do? How be a Jew? Why be a Jew?

III

The answer was slow in coming. I could not invent it ; it had to be sought for, and sought for right down the long history of Israel, from the legendary days of the Bible to the last hours of the present time. Such a task demanded years, perhaps a whole life. I was like Taine, faced with the necessity of voting, and finding himself bound to write the *Origines de la France Contemporaine* before he could make up his mind. But I was not Taine. I lacked the necessary courage. I felt the pull of other ambitions, which required less austerity. I was attracted by literature and the theatre, and I could not resist their appeal. But always it came back to me, the question without an answer: How be a Jew? Why be a Jew ? And always with it came the pricking of my conscience at the laziness in me that had not found the answer.

The years went by. I often saw my dear Logician. Passing from nationalism to royalism his thought had developed harmoniously, and, comparing it with the disorder of my own, I suffered. Every morning I read, in a paper which still appears, two articles: one expounded, in the calm phrases of a perfect style, the doctrine of total nationalism : the other, with a wonderfully ingenious improvisation of ludicrous epithets, translated this doctrine into insults. These insults were, nearly all of them, addressed to the Jews ; and, being addressed to the Jews, they were addressed to me. Every morning I read this paper ; every morning I swore never to read it again ; and every morning I read it just the same. And every morning the reading of it left me in a state of fury and distress.

I married. I had a son, whose son you will be, my child. And then a strange thing happened. By chance, the morning my son was born, I did not read this paper. And I have never read it since. Why did the birth of this son free me from this obsession ? I did not know. But, when he was one year old, something else happened, no less surprising. A play of mine had just been put on with some success ; everything prompted me to persevere. I abandoned it all and for three years, without respite, I studied Judaism.

I think I understand now the power that impelled me,

and the moment it chose for its purpose. Already, no doubt, I was obeying the instinct that is dictating this book for you today : I would not instruct my children in the religion of my fathers, and yet I wished to hand on to them something of Israel.

Is there an ancestral memory ? I can hardly doubt it ; for I had the constant sense then that what I was learning I was not learning but remembering. First Hebrew. Oh, I shall never know it as I would ! But I already know it well enough to be persuaded that it is impossible to understand Israel without understanding Hebrew. Those words with the strange syllables which I had so often heard during my childhood, those words whose meaning had remained closed to me, now suddenly threw themselves open before me, like doors that might open on to treasure. And it was not only their meaning which illumined me, but also the soul that breathed through them. A whole world, that of my father, that of myself, was reflected there, in the clear connection between derivatives from a common root, in the rudimentary structure of the sentence, in the illogical incoherence of the imagery, in the powerlessness to express pure abstraction, in the vague contours of the verb which, hardly distinguishing past, present, and future, seems to move in eternity.

I wished to know the religious thought of Israel. Better than any commentary, some notes, written in the course of my reading, will make clear to you my wariness at the time of this discovery, and what were my surprises and my joys :

The chosen people ! The mission of Israel ! . . What absurdities ! . . Should Israel have a mission, and the others not ? Why ?

*   *   *   *

They want a God all to themselves : the God of Abraham, of Isaac, and of Jacob, the God of Israel ! He makes an *alliance* with the patriarchs ! He renews it on Sinai with their descendants ! A pact unites the Eternal to this people, for eternity ! . . .

What then is this God ? An idol ? A fetish ? The God of a tribe of savages ? The private God of Israel ?. . .

But no: he calls the Egyptians his people, he calls the Assyrians the work of his hands ; the prophets of the Gentiles have knowledge of him ; the Talmud forbids one to interrupt idolaters in prayer before their idols, for it is this God whom they are addressing without knowing it. Before speaking to Israel this God spoke to Noah, and gave commandments to all the human families ; he created heaven and earth. He is the One God, the God of all men, the God of the whole world. Then why the *God of Israel* ?

I don't understand.

* * * *

And their Torah, that law which separates them from all peoples ! They do not plough as others do : Moses forbids them to yoke to the same plough an ass and an ox ; they do not sow as others do : Moses forbids them to sow the same field with two kinds of seed ; they do not reap or gather, build or reckon, eat or pray as others do ; they keep themselves distinct by the fashion of their garments, by not rounding the corners of their heads nor shaving the corners of their beards, by the token of the covenant in their flesh.

To separate a people from all humanity : intolerable pride !. . .

And this same Law, we are to believe, contains the eternal Wisdom ? To break it would be to disturb the order of the universe ? God consulted it when he created the worlds ? God himself studies the Torah ?

I don't understand.

* * * *

Their sages say : the Bible *speaks in the language of men.* Undoubtedly they mean by this that God revealed even to the prophets only what they could understand of him, and in language that they could understand. This would explain and justify at a stroke all the anthropomorphisms of the Holy Scriptures.

* * * *

Moses at the school of Akiba : what beautiful symbolism in this talmudic tale ! God shows to Moses, before his death, his disciple Akiba, who will live nearly a century after Jesus Christ. The prophet sits in the last of the eight rows at the school of Akiba and listens while the rabbi teaches. Akiba

comments on the Law of Moses, Moses does not recognise it ;
nevertheless, it is the Law of Moses.

So the divine revelation, received by the patriarchs and
prophets, continues, it would seem, in the tradition, and
this continued revelation, like the first, speaks to each
generation only in language that it can understand ; its
expression develops, and purifies itself, with the growth of
human knowledge.

The Bible, then, does not suffice. Just as the New Testament does not hold the whole of Catholicism, so the Old
does not hold the whole of Judaism. I must get to know the
two Talmuds, the Zohar, Yehuda Halevi, Gabirol, Maimon-
ides, all the great thinkers, all the great doctors of the
Synagogue. Otherwise I shall know nothing.

*　　　*　　　*　　　*

I used to believe this Jewish God inaccessible, clothing
his omnipotence in cloud and thunder, so as to keep it far
from mortals. And here, in the tender outpourings of the
psalms, I find him again as close as long ago in my childish
prayer. The patriarchs speak to him almost familiarly ;
Abraham bargains with him. Akiba, Ben Zakkai, Nahum of
Gimso, Rabbi Chanina, Rabbi Meir, all the sages of Israel
live in friendship with him. Between this God and man is
there need of a mediator ?

*　　　*　　　*　　　*

I am again astonished. Jesus forgives the sinner who
repents, and him who *knows not what he does*; but he whips the
money-changers out of the Temple, and curses the wicked
Pharisees in language as violent as that of the prophets.
The God who punishes is not absent, then, from the New
Testament ?

Can it be that the God who pardons is to be found in
the Old ?

*　　　*　　　*　　　*

Yes, he is there ! The God of Israel, the God of justice and
vengeance is also the Father, the God of love and forgiveness. He forgives to the thousandth generation ; even his
justice is mingled with mercy ; he punishes only when the
measure is full to overflowing and when punishment alone
can teach remorse and penitence ; and a contrite heart is
more pleasing in his sight than all the offerings of the earth.

And if the history of Israel is a history of his punishments, it is also, and still more, a history of his forgiveness.

*   *   *   *

" Thou shalt love the Lord thy God with all thine heart, and with all thy soul, and with all thy might."

This sentence, quoted by Jesus, is from Moses !

*   *   *   *

What ? The whole of the Lord's Prayer ? . . . *Our Father which art in Heaven . . . Hallowed be thy name . . . Thy Kingdom come . . . Thy will be done in earth, as it is in heaven . . . Give us our daily bread . . . Forgive us our trespasses . . . Lead us not into temptation.* Every one of these phrases, spoken by Jesus in his prayer, is a Jewish phrase !

*   *   *   *

What then can be the difference between Judaism and Christianity ? Love of one's neighbour, I have been told : a great Christian discovery ?

No. The Hebrew of old times must be gentle to his slave and must free him with compensation after six years : he must give back before sunset the coat taken in pledge : he must leave some sheaves in his field for the poor, the widow and the orphan : he must love the stranger like a brother.

The Jew of the talmudic period must open his door to the poor as if he were one of his own family ; he must be charitable to Jews and non-Jews, honour the old, whether Jews or non-Jews, and bury the dead and comfort those who mourn them, whether Jews or non-Jews.

" Thou shalt love thy neighbour as thyself." This phrase is also from Moses.

*   *   *   *

And this is how the Talmud speaks of the unity of man :

" Whoever pities his fellow is a descendant of Abraham." " Why did God, at the time of creation, make only one man ? For the sake of peace ; so that no man could ever after say to another ' I am of older race than you.' "

*   *   *   *

Is it then perhaps belief in the future life and the Last Judgement that distinguishes the one religion from the other ? A belief which I do not find in the five books of Moses ?

But Job declares that, when freed from the flesh, he will

see God. In Daniel's vision those who sleep in the dust will awaken, some to splendour and some to shame. All Jewish prayers are addressed to the God " who quickens the dead " ; all the Jewish Apocalypses evoke the Day of the Great Judgement ; all the Jewish doctors live in the expectation of eternal life.

Then who or what separates you, Jews and Christians ?

*   *   *   *

The Messiah ! The Messiah ! According to the Christians he has come ; the Jews await him still !

*   *   *   *

Who was he then, this promised Messiah ? The Anointed of God, the ideal King of Israel, on whom shall rest the Spirit of the Lord. He shall not judge after the sight of his eyes, neither reprove after the hearing of his ears ; but with righteousness shall he judge the poor, and reprove with equity for the meek of the earth.

After suffering with his people, and taking on himself the sins of the world, he shall lead Israel back from the four corners of the universe, and shall give her a dominion wholly of the spirit. In the last days, the mountain of Zion shall be established in the top of the mountains, and the peoples shall flow unto it, and they shall say " Come ye, and let us go up to the mountain of the Lord, to the house of the God of Jacob ; and he will teach us his ways, and we will walk in his paths : for out of Zion shall go forth the law, and the word of the Lord from Jerusalem."

And all the peoples shall beat their swords into plowshares, and their spears into pruninghooks : nation shall not lift up sword against nation, neither shall they learn war any more. " For the Lord hath spoken it."

That was the promise. Did Jesus keep it ?

*   *   *   *

He believed that the end of the world was near. He said : "Thy kingdom come." And he believed that it had come, this kingdom of justice and love and peace. And he believed himself this Messiah, bringing to the world peace, love and justice.

But the Jews, looking round them, still saw injustice, war and hate, and they went on waiting.

Then, that their faith might accord with the prophecies, the Christians spoke of a second coming, of which the prophets had in fact never spoken, and of a return of their Messiah, by which everything would be finally accomplished.

To await his return, is not that to await his coming ?

* * * *

Poor crucified Jesus, for whom my childhood wept, belovèd Jesus, whose blood-stained face I can never see, in the darkness of some chapel, without trembling, were you then wrong ? And was your error a blasphemy ? You yourself said that no letter of the Law could be changed, and that it was holy. It was this Law which condemned you. Was it in holiness, then, that it condemned you ? And if so, what was the crime of those Jews who, in your own words, knew not what they did, and who, rather than greet you as the Eternal submitting to death, the Unlimited limiting itself in human form, the visible Son of the Invisible, were ready to shed the blood of the purest of their sons, and to let the indelible mark of it flow over them for ever and ever ?

* * * *

Between these Hebrew dreamers and the Greek thinkers, what a gulf ! The Greeks proceed by subtle reasoning, the Hebrews by massive intuition.

At first sight, the reasoning appears to be the more convincing : an illusion of discursive thought. Does it not itself rest no less on masked intuitions which it assumes as axioms, and which do not of themselves possess any logical validity ?

And why prefer in principle, and apart from specific application, reasoning to intuition ?

* * * *

" Hear, O Israel : the Lord our God, the Lord is One."

In the ages when men, separated from one another, bowed down before thousands of gods, and saw in nature the action of the thousand separate forces of these thousand separate gods, they had this astonishing intuition of the One God, those old Hebrew prophets.

And science today is rediscovering this unity in the universe, and is showing me, in the structure of the atom and of the solar system, a single plan and a single thought.

* * * *

I read in the Talmud that God created man and that " man is free," and in the Zohar that " the word of man creates new heavens."

Creation, liberty : two ideas foreign to Greek thought, but the substance of Jewish. God, creator and free, creates man in his own image ; and man, freely created in the image of God, creates freely in his turn !

*   *   *   *

God, say these Jews, is at once outside the world and in it. Outside the world, transcendant, he is inaccessible to human thought. In the world, immanent, he is very near to us, he is in us. And in so much as it is in us, this divine Presence, this Shekhina, as they call it, is bound up, so to say, with the movement of human consciousness. The unity of God, refracted in the diversity of creatures, is broken ; it is divided in the divisions of men ; but prayer and justice, which unite men, can re-establish it.

A doctor of the Talmud tells us that in the first days the Presence of God dwelt here below ; Adam's sin caused it to go up to the first heaven, Cain's to the second ; with the generation of Enoch, and those of the Flood, Babel, Sodom and Egypt, it went up, heaven by heaven, to the seventh. But the virtues of Abraham, Isaac, Jacob, Levi, Kohath and Amram brought it down, heaven by heaven, to the first ; and, with Moses, it returned to earth.

According to the Zohar, when men glorify God on earth, the angels glorify him in heaven ; when men sin on earth, they silence the angels' hymns in heaven ; when they proclaim the Unity of God on earth, they make it real in all the worlds.

In this way man's justice would increase and strengthen the Presence of God on earth. Man would collaborate with God. Creating anew the world created by God, he would complete it. His sin would shatter the divine unity ; his goodness would give back God's unity to God.

That is the whole of Jewish mysticism. It is not lacking in grandeur.

*   *   *   *

Is it then inadmissible, this God hypothesis ?

I cannot explain the movement of the hands on my watch apart from the intelligence that conceived the mechanism

nd the will that executed it ; and should I explain the
omplex harmony of the universe by the play of chance and
olind forces ? Am I not bound to suppose that there exists
omewhere something in the nature of an intelligence and
will infinitely more powerful than those of man, and that
oy it everything can be explained ?

I have long since renounced the puerile atheism, and
even the agnosticism, of my first philosophical ambitions.
Spencer and Kant are now alike powerless to influence me.
no longer believe that spirit can come from matter,
evolution or no evolution, if matter has not first received
spirit. I no longer believe that reality is utterly unknowable ;
o feel it unknowable is already in some fashion to know it ;
and if we are able, when thinking it, to impose on it the
orms of our thought, then there must be, between our
hought and reality, some relation of harmony.

The great savants of today inform me that science
tself is nothing but a vast hypothesis, which merely ex-
olains provisionally and approximately certain aspects of
eality. If the God hypothesis explains to me some other
aspects of it, must I reject it just because it is only a
hypothesis ? Does not the secular, godless philosophy of
Lachelier, of Boutroux, of Henri Poincaré end, with Berg-
son, in *the fact of liberty*, in *the reality of the spirit*, in *the idea
of a God creative and free* ? And is not that precisely the
thought of Israel ?

How often have I surprised myself reasoning, quite in-
voluntarily, as if, without knowing it, I accepted the
presence in me of this Spirit ! How often has some event in
 my life been made clear to me not by the events that pre-
ceded it but by those that followed, as if some hidden providence, with which I had collaborated of my own free will,
had prepared my future in my past, and had brought me to
t by my own act !

If this Spirit is really present in me and in the world,
must it not be present also in the history of the world ? In
the history of the nations, in the history of Israel ? One
might then conceive that certain intelligences, certain races
had felt its presence more clearly than others, and that the
people which felt it, so they believed, most clearly, had also
felt the mission to proclaim it.

Why not ?

*   *   *   *

A Jewish race ?

Every anthropological type, it appears, is to be foun
in Israel : brachycephalic Jews, dolichocephalic Jews ; whi
Jews, yellow Jews, black Jews.

Perhaps, then, Israel is a race only spiritually ? Perha[
these many bloods form a single blood only because o
thought flows in them ?

*   *   *   *

The Torah of Israel. I begin to see more clearly. Tw
aspects of the Torah :

1. The moral and religious precepts of order, justic
peace and love which are the ideal law of all human societ
and are also the law of the universe ; for, according to ou
prophets and sages, the order that presides over the ha
mony of the earth and skies is of the same essence as th
moral order. (And this must be why : " God, when crea
ing the world, read the Torah.")

2. The law peculiar to Israel : it includes the other, bu
adds to it all the ordinances that regulate the life of th
people and make it a people different from other peoples.

Between these two aspects of the Torah, a close tie ; i
order that, at the end of days, the Messiah may reign o
earth with his justice, his peace and his love, it is necessar
that Israel, who is the hope of the Messiah, should remai
Israel to the end of days. Her special law, then, must b
eternal, like the universal law.

*   *   *   *

How unjust I was to those six hundred and thirteen obse
vances demanded of a Jew ! The religious customs that
had criticised in my adolescence suddenly shine for me wit
the light of a magnificent meaning.

It was a question, for these Jews, of associating Go
with every act of life, the humblest as well as the highest
of making each of these acts a service to God : and b
spiritualising in this way even eating and drinking, o
transposing our daily existence on to a spiritual plane.

It was a question, by ritual, by charity, by penitence, b
feasts, by joy, of creating, as the Bible says, a nation o
priests : not of priests cut off from life by prayer and con

mplation, but of priests accepting and living life in all its
rms, in study, in work, in the family, and in society, and
nctifying every act of this life by prayer and contempla-
ɔn. A people composed entirely of men like my father.
'hat a people !

*   *   *   *

And that is not all. Israel wished to be a holy people not
r herself alone, but also for her mission.

Her mission ! Egoism ? Pride ? Not in the hearts of our
ophets and sages ! To them Israel is a base and wretched
ɔple, loaded with sins and for ever backsliding. God chose
ιis mire only to show what he can do with mire. For this
od of Israel in no way belongs to Israel : he is the God whom
rael must reveal to all mankind. Amid the hostility of the
ɔples, this people must proclaim the name of the One God,
ιtil the day comes when all peoples will join with it in
loring the One God.

In thus taking on herself the burden of her Law, Israel
els herself chosen not as a master but as a servant : she
ɛeps herself so far from others only as a duty self-imposed :
ιe separates herself from others only to unite them.

*   *   *   *

Two aspects of this mission :

1. To proclaim throughout the world the Name of the
ne God.

2. To hope, to wait and to work for the reign of justice
ιd peace on earth with the coming of the Messiah.

Faith in One God, Messianism : between these two ideas
there a link ?

*   *   *   *

I see ! I see ! My search is finished ! I understand ! " Love
ιe Lord thy God." " Love thy neighbour as thyself." These
vo commandments, say our doctors with Jesus, are really
ιe : man being the image of God, to love man is to love
od.

" Be holy, as I am holy " says the Eternal to the He-
rews. Man, created in the image of God, must resemble his
·eator.

Now God is One, man ought to be One. By his divisions
ere on earth he shatters the divine Unity. To proclaim that

Unity is not then sufficient. " If you wish to glorify God " says the Talmud " try to be like him." That the Kingdom o God may come, man, created by God, must be recreated by man, until human unity reflects and reconstructs in thi world the unity of God.

According to the talmudic and cabbalistic commentar on Genesis, Adam, image of God, was originally at once mal and female : conjugal love, a return to this unity, is alread a return to the image of the divine unity. Sin has multiplied men and divided them : the love of family, the love of one' neighbour, social justice, which create, by union, greater and greater human groups, create greater and greater images o the divine unity : and the peace of the nations will create the greatest of all these images. " The name of the Lord i Peace " : when men, as free creators, have created Man "The Lord shall be One, and his Name One."

Belief in the progress of mankind, creating by its pro gress the Kingdom of God, that is the faith of Israel. The practice of her Law seems to her linked with the coming of the Messiah, and the coming of the Messiah with that of perfec man. To accomplish this promise, she wishes to educate her self, to preserve herself, to make of herself, as the Talmud says, "a cement" between the peoples, to take into herself in the words of Yehuda Halevi, "the heart of the world" identifying, alone among all, her destiny with the destiny of all, she wishes to become a people of priests, that she may become the priest of humanity.

Human Unity is not, then, for Israel a logical entity, but a revealed truth, a divine truth, which is projected on to the future from the past, and which the people that proclaims it must make, down the ages, and with the other peoples, a human reality.

Human Unity is for the Jew an article of faith, like the divine Unity ; and when I try to find, in the consciousness o my race, what is my duty as a Jew, God answers me " You duty as a Jew is your duty as a man."

You see, my child, how far I was from my Logician : rea soning outside the Jewish faith, he seemed to me to oppose humanity to his race ; a Jew, I had to mingle mine and humanity.

ISRAEL EVERLASTING

That these ideas were admirable I had no doubt. But in what measure was I going to adopt them ? They might be nothing but beautiful fancies.

Nevertheless, if my intelligence preserved its critical attitude, my heart was touched. What perspectives were opening out ! What a past, and what a future ! The dream of this people was perhaps an illusion : but what a place the very illusion gave to this people in the world, and what a place it gave to me also, descended from this people !

What the intelligence of the philosopher might still doubt —and I was already no longer a philosopher—the imagination of the poet, which I would have desired to be, dared to affirm. I wished to dedicate to my father's memory that lived in my heart a sort of Jewish *Légende des siècles*, which would be, from antiquity to the present day, the epic of the great mission. So were written the poems that make up the first two books of *Ecoute Israël*.

I drew on the fables of the Talmud. God, as he saw how men would sin and hate, hesitated, in my pages, to create the world : then Abraham, Isaac and Jacob, the three heroes without arms and without an army, rose into his thought, and for them he said " Let there be light." I told of Egypt, of the warriors and priests accusing the Hebrews before Pharaoh, of the River of Sobs and the grievous Bush, and of Moses, on the threshold of the Promised Land and begging that he might live to enter into it, and God showing him another Promised Land, the Land that will be when One Man will be. And I followed the Promise, from Samson to Gideon, from Samuel to David ; I built the Temple of Solomon for peace ; I saw Jezebel and Zedekiah, Elijah and Jeremiah ; I lived again those sins and those forgivenesses, and the punished people dragging itself into exile, and God putting the fetter on his neck and the

shackles on his hands that he might follow his people o
their bloody road to human unity.

And I was going to sing the captive songs of Babylor
Ezekiel and Nehemiah, the hope of return—when tl
great war broke out. Will you understand, my child, wha
it was that happened to me then? I had just hear
within me all the lyricism of my race : Israel had brought m
back to live in Israel—and here again, as once at Basle in tl
midst of the Zionists, I felt myself Jewish, very Jewish, bu
also very French. I had to give myself with a giving tha
was instinctive, immediate and total ; and, as I was sti
a citizen of Geneva, I enlisted in the Foreign Legion an
left for the front : that is why, if you are born, my chil
you will be born a Frenchman.

It was natural enough ; ten thousand Jews in France, les
French than I, did what I did; and I should not be speakin
of it now had it not raised for me a new question, and th
one I had least expected : how could I feel myself at on
more Jewish and more French ? How was it that Germa
Jews in Germany, Russian Jews in Russia, Jews of ever
country in every country, were no doubt feeling what
was feeling ? That is the Jewish mystery of today ; and :
was only later that I solved it.

Be reassured, my child : I am not going to give an ac
count of the war, not even of *my* war (which, after two year:
brought me back to a government office in Paris). You nee
only know how great was the human hope that shon
through so many horrors.

We were told : this is the last war. And we hoped an
believed that it was the last war. I sometimes thought of i
standing in a trench, and looking out, under the smoke c
the distant shells, over the tiny bit of the world that coul
be seen through the narrow slit of a loophole ; and I woul
see in imagination all the countries, all the continents, an
everywhere, anxious, confident, men, all men, hoping
waiting for the end of the last war, and for the peace of th
whole world, the Unity of man.

And I said to myself : Then it did not cry in the wilder
ness, the voice of the prophets ? The dream once dreamed b
dreamers of Judæa has become the dream of all humanity
All men, then, are awaiting the Messiah of Israel ? How :

hat possible ? By what miracle has the message of Israel
ome to them ? The mission ? Might it be by the mission of
srael ?

And I was already writing in my thoughts the last song
f the Jewish epic, *Le Mur des Pleurs*. The Wandering Jew
topped before the old wall where the Jews were lamenting
ver the ruins of the Temple ; but they were not bewailing
he Temple that had been destroyed ; they were bewailing
he Temple of the One Man, which man has not yet built.
'he Wandering Jew slept ; and, in the visions of the night,
e saw the whole war ; he died all the deaths of all the
oldiers, by shot, by gas, by submarine, by aeroplane. All
he mothers of the great war wept for their sons, all the dead
f the great war raised from the tomb their rotted hands,
nd cursed, with their shattered mouths, the Antichrist
ho was arming their bones for a war of the dead in eternity.

And now, breaking in on the dream, come distant chants.
'uture generations are building the long awaited Temple,
or from fratricide is born fraternity. They are bringing, for
he Bread, the wheat of all the fields : they are bringing, for
he Wine, the grapes of all the vines : the Table is set on all
he mountains, all the plains, all the oceans. All the races go
p and take their places ; the Holy Supper of humanity
egins ; the limbs of Adam, scattered over the earth, are
ined once more ; the blood of all men flows in his veins ;
a his heart beat all human hearts ; as God, Man is One.

But voices lament anew. The Wandering Jew awakes. At
he foot of the ruined wall the Jews are still weeping : the
mes are not yet come, he must wander still.

And I also awoke from my dream of the great war, and
o did the whole world : peace was not peace : war was still
ar : men wept : the Jews wept.

They had fought, the Jews, for every nation : every na-
on had inscribed in the book of its glories Jewish heroism
nd Jewish loyalty, and the image of Israel torn asunder
as, more than ever, the image of humanity. But while my
ussian-Jewish comrades of the Legion and their brothers
f the Russian front were dying *for* the Tsar, their fathers,
heir wives and their children, accused of treason, im-
risoned as hostages, driven over the highways through the

night and snow, knouted, shot, hanged, burned alive, wer
dying in Russia *by* the Tsar.

After the Bolshevik revolution it was still worse. In th
silence of my nights I no longer heard the groan of one dis
honoured captain on his rock in the sea : the cry that wen
up brought me hundreds of thousands of agonies, even mor
pitiable than those of the great war. From my sleepless bed
saw the counter-revolutionary armies of Petlura, of Gots
chalk and of Denikin : I watched them advance, shoutin
"The Jews are Bolsheviks ! The Bolsheviks are Jews ! '
and throwing themselves on the unarmed Jews, torturin
them, mutilating them, cutting them down in the street:
and gouging out, in the cellars, the eyes of their childrer
From Germany to Hungary, from Austria to Rumania, th
cry was repeated : " The Jews are Bolsheviks, the Bolshevik
are Jews. They willed the evil war ! They signed the ev
peace ! Death to the Jews ! Death to the Jews ! ". An
while a new exodus of Israel passed, in rags and winding
sheets, through the capitals of Europe, and crossed the ocea
in anguish, to find the ports of America closed to them
all the old antisemitic calumnies, all the murderous fable
spread across the world in a flood of print.

How was it possible ? All these Jewish heroes who ha
died for all these countries were, then, forgotten ? All thes
bloody proofs of all these patriotisms had, then, proved no
thing ? What was the cause of this hatred of the Jew, whic
nothing appeases, which has existed ever since Jews hav
existed, and which will no doubt endure as long as the
endure ?

I wanted to know. I set myself to read these indictment
and to compare them with the history of Israel, with whic
the preparation of my *Jewish Anthology* was making m
more familiar. I made up my mind to discover the caus€
beyond all dispute, of antisemitism. Might not its dis
covery complete, perhaps, my knowledge of Judaism ?

I had quickly to discard a number of well-known myth:
such as that of ritual murder; which is still persistentl
represented as an authentic Jewish practice, when the li
has been given to the thing a hundred times, even by th
Popes ; or the traditional picture of the rapacious Jew, whic
Shakespeare has immortalised in his Shylock, unaware tha

in the original legend this pitiless creditor is not a Jew, and that the right to claim a piece of flesh from an insolvent debtor goes back, not to the law of Moses, but to the wholly Roman law of the Twelve Tables.

I had also to neglect arguments drawn from certain talmudic texts, mere isolated opinions contrary to the general thought of the Talmud and of Judaism itself, but which our traducers would make into articles of faith binding on all Jews.

Finally I had to exclude so-called Christian antisemitism. Christ commanded that the Jews should be forgiven; in the doctrine of St. Paul, which the Church inherited, their very crime had an element of holiness, for it was the beginning, through Jesus' sacrifice, of the salvation of the world ; and they must live to the end of time, to finish their mission by converting through their example the pagans of the last days. If Christians have persecuted Jews (and they have done so horribly and do so still), that is because they have neither Christian virtues nor Christian beliefs ; they remain pagan ; one cannot be antisemitic without being antichristian.

Then what serious complaints could I retain ?

Is it true that Judaism is *in its essence revolutionary* ? If moral, social and international progress means revolution, yes : no, if revolution means violence. Karl Marx, a Jew baptised at the age of six and an antisemite at the age of reason, formulated, it is true, the theory of communism, which, with its noble passion for the disinherited, is in the prophetic tradition ; but, so far as concerns the translation of this sentiment into terms of revolution, it is easy to show that *historical materialism*, which is essential to Marxism, is the total negation of *historical spiritualism*, which is essential to Judaism, and that communism has its origins in the socialism of Proudhon, Louis Blanc, Saint-Simon, and Babeuf, who, if they were Jews, knew how to conceal it.

In the Mosaic legislation the soil belongs not to the State but to God, and it is inalienable, in the sense that a piece of land can be sold only for a certain time, after which it returns by law to its former holders. This conservative measure makes a lasting inequality of wealth impossible, and far from provoking revolution tends to prevent it ; and no Jewish tradition either enjoins or permits the imposition of the measure itself, anywhere whatsoever, by revolutionary violence.

Is not the Talmud filled with conservative maxims ? " Woe to the ship that has lost its pilot, woe to the society that has lost its guide." " Always respect the higher authority of your country." " If the king orders you to turn a mountain upside down, set yourself to the work without murmuring." Does not the tenth commandment, by forbidding us to covet the goods of others, condemn, in its very thought, the class struggle ? Was it not in the Bible that Bossuet found his *Politique tirée de l'Ecriture Sainte* which establishes the divine right of kings ? Before leaving Egypt and their bondage, did not the Hebrews await the assent of Pharaoh ? Did not the Jews allow themselves to be butchered for eighteen hundred years without revolting, without even defending themselves ? Must they not almost cease to be Jews before they will at last take up arms against the pogroms ?

Then Judaism is perhaps *in its essence capitalist* ? But every word of the Bible and the Talmud exalts poverty ; the moment they are able, the Jews desert business for intellectual culture ; everywhere, except when the doors are closed to them by iniquitous legislation, as in Rumania and Hungary, they flock to the Universities in quite disproportionate numbers ; by the side of the great Christian capitalists the great Jewish capitalists cut a poor figure; the Jewish proletariat is the most wretched of all proletariats

Or can it be that Judaism is an international organisation, designed to conquer for the Jews material supremacy and world empire, as promised by their sacred books ? But the persecutions undergone by so many Jews during so many centuries, and in the century in which we are living, prove the absence among them of an effective solidarity and their lack of even a defensive organisation ; and the world empire which the prophets announce is to be built, not by a financial conspiracy, but by the triumph of an effort wholly spiritual, which will have led all mankind to its highest degree of development.

Finally, what validity can be given to antisemitic arguments when one sees Henry Ford, the richest man in the world and the most independent, first for ten years subsidising antisemitism both in Europe and in America, and then publicly recanting and publicly asking the Jews' forgiveness ?

But how could this honourable man have been so misled? Out of so many contradictory accusations does nothing, then, remain ?

Yes. One fact, without justifying these accusations, explains them all : the Jews are Jews ; they wish to remain Jews ; always, everywhere, even in spite of themselves, they remain Jews.

Now every minority seems suspect to the majority, which holds that members of the minority are more like one another, and show greater solidarity, than members of the majority. Must a culprit be found at all cost ? Then look for him in the minority, and accuse the whole of it. One Jew is a traitor, all Jews are traitors; a hundred Jews are Bolsheviks, all Jews are Bolsheviks; the plague rages in the Middle Ages, the Jews have poisoned the wells ; war rages in the twentieth century, the Jews have plotted the war.

This phenomenon of collective and half deliberate illusion is incontestable : poisoning of wells, use of human blood, sorcery and magic, all the accusations launched against the Jews of the Middle Ages by the Christians, who had become the majority, are precisely those which the pagans, ten centuries before, were hurling at the Christians, then a minority.

Socially, politically, economically, there exists between a Jewish and a non-Jewish capitalist no difference ; but in fact, or by his origins of which he always preserves some trace, the Jewish capitalist is a Jew : he belongs to a minority ; he strikes the attention, he stands out from the rest ; one sees only him, one wishes to see only him ; and, if one has a complaint against capitalists, one calls them Jews. Financiers or savants, industrialists or philosophers, dramatists or statesmen, conservatives or revolutionaries, there are Jews everywhere : they can be accused of everything ; and so indeed they are.

I had come, then, to think that there was only one real cause of antisemitism: the claim of Jews to be Jews. But was the claim justified ? By what right had this people been able to defend it throughout the centuries, and, even today, to make it prevail ? To deserve, in my eyes, this exorbitant favour of remaining apart while mingling with the rest, Israel must be necessary, her mission must seem to me not merely a beautiful dream of prophets or a beautiful theme for a poem, but a verifiable reality. I had sung of this mission with all my heart : was I going to believe in it with all my mind ? And, if so, whither would this faith lead me ?

Only the history of Israel could give me the answer. This history, like all others, begins with legend: but what should I think of it if I found it as miraculous in its authentic developments as in its legendary origins ?

A shepherd of Chaldæa dreams under the stars, near his sleeping flocks. A voice says to him : " I am the God of heaven and earth. Leave thy country and the idols of thy father, and go to the country which I shall show thee. I will make of thee a great nation and in thee shall all families of the earth be blessed." A race springs from him, which lives in bondage on the banks of the Nile, for to do its work this race must know every sorrow. Moses frees them, leads them to dwell in the wilderness for forty years, gives them a Law which forbids murder, theft, lying, blasphemy, lust, covetousness—which commands them to love God and their neighbour—which rules the life of this horde in justice, peace and charity so that it may become a people of saints.

And now the horde is in the land that was promised to it. It is a nation ; it has kings. But Israel is unworthy of her Law ; ceaselessly she falls and falls again into idolatry ; and that is for her the sin that includes all others, for the living faith in a God that is One, invisible and spiritual is the first of the truths which she owes to the world. Her prophets tell her that she will perish if she denies her God ; and her God, turn by turn, punishes her and pardons her, as she observes or neglects her Law.

She splits up into two kingdoms. The one defiles itself with the lust and slaughter of idolatry, and never repents; it forgets its God, its God forgets it; it is conquered and carried away ; it disappears from the world. The other, which is also guilty, goes captive to Babylon ; but its God has remained in the heart of its prophets its God and the God of all men,

for all men were created in his image, and it is for all men
that his people shall give birth, such is his will, to the Messiah
of peace and justice, who shall mould the unity of man from
the unity of God. And see how this people, repenting, finds its
reward : Cyrus, a pagan king, gives it back the land of its
ancestors ; it returns there, cleansed of idolatry ; neither
Greece with her beauty nor Rome with her power can turn
it any more from its God. But it is torn by inner hatreds and
perishes in a second exile, which disperses it to the four
corners of the earth : its first Temple, destroyed as a punishment for idolatry, had been rebuilt for the divine Unity ; its
second Temple, destroyed as a punishment for strife, must
be rebuilt for human Unity.

And now, as the prophets foretold, the truth of Israel
begins to spread.   Jesus, one of the purest of her sons, proclaimed it in the most moving language, believing that the
end of the world was at hand and that he himself was the
awaited Messiah. But justice and peace have not yet come :
Israel still waits. And the Christians deify their prophet, and
the pagans, accustomed to visible gods, believe that they
see with their eyes the invisible God of Israel : and so
Christian truth is for the Jews only a half-truth.

The Roman Empire becomes Christian. It commands the
Jews to become Christians. They await their Messiah. Meanwhile, the destruction of the Temple has lost to them the
centre of their religious life ; but they build it anew in the
Synagogue and in the School, and spiritualise it still more in
their affliction. Torn from the soil of their fatherland, they
make of their Law an ideal fatherland, linking to the fulfil-
ment of the promises it holds for them and for all mankind
the hope of their ultimate return.

Once again a new thought breaks off from the ancient
thought of Israel : Mohammed preaches to the Arabs the God
of Abraham : and while, in its Christian form, this God will
conquer, after Europe, the two Americas, in its Mussulman
form it conquers Africa, and Asia as far as the borders of
China. But Mohammed encircles him with martial pomp
and a sensual paradise, where the Jews no longer recognise
the God of Israel ; and so the truth of Islam, like that of
Christ, is for them only a half-truth.

Then, down the ages, wherever they live, the heirs of

Judaism persecute the Jews. Justinian deprives them of civil equality and religious liberty. Sisebut the Visigoth and Dagobert the Frank offer them the choice of exile or baptism. The Crusaders massacre them, the Turks massacre them, the Moroccans massacre them, the Russians massacre them. They are driven out of France ; they are driven out of England ; they are driven out of Spain ; flogged, tortured, they await their Messiah.

But, however great their misery, however numerous their exiles, in every age Providence finds them a shelter. First in Babylonia, under the Parthian domination : they found their Academies, they write their Talmuds. Then in Andalusia, in Sicily, in Castille, in Aragon, at Narbonne, at Carcassonne, at Spire, at Pavia, in Rome : they create a poetry and a philosophy ; they translate Greek thinkers for Christian thinkers ; they give counsel to kings and attend on Popes, and they accompany Columbus across the Atlantic. Then, in Holland, from their ancient mysticism springs a modern philosophy, and, in Poland, a new mysticism from their old religion.

Meanwhile, Luther and Calvin have re-read the Bible, and criticism is born : at the time of Jesus the Jews said " Jesus is not God," and they waited. Twenty centuries after Jesus half Christendom will say " Jesus was not God," and they will return to the One God of Israel.

Meanwhile, Rousseau has dreamed, Robespierre has spoken, Karl Marx has written, Wilson has preached. Ten centuries, twenty centuries perhaps before Jesus, the Hebrews said " The oppressed is thy brother : the poor is thy brother : the stranger is thy brother : Man, like God, is One." And they waited. Twenty centuries after Jesus, man marches towards his unity.

But, here still, the world has taken from Israel only half her truth ; for not Robespierre, nor Karl Marx, nor Wilson repeats in its purity the message of the prophets. However nobly they may wish to approach the prophetic ideal, they still keep it far from them, shut up in a prison-house of matter.

Assuredly, for Israel, the moral and social duties of the privileged to the disinherited, and of nations to one another, are not optional but absolutely binding : the Hebrew word

that is translated by " charity " means in Hebrew " justice,"
and this justice must reign over individuals and peoples.
But, by the same token, the code of Israel is a code of duties,
not of rights or interests. It says to the oppressor " You owe
his liberty to the oppressed " : it does not say to the oppressed " You may oppress the oppressor." It says to the
rich " You owe your riches to the poor " : it does not say to
the poor " You may plunder the rich." It says to the nations
" Lay down your arms " : but it also says to them " Put love
in your hearts."

Israel utters, down the ages, her word of Unity ; the
word, as it is uttered, becomes reality ; but, in becoming
reality, it becomes dim ; and Israel must keep it clear, so as
to say it and say it again, in all its clarity, to the end of time.

Just as Christianity, by incarnating the divine Unity in
the flesh of a man, and then Mohammedanism, by ascribing
to it violent or sensual promises, robbed it in some degree of
its spirituality to render it accessible, so Jacobinism,
Marxism and Wilsonism popularise human Unity only in a
form that is still confused and superficial ; these are the
stages on a road which seeks, from without, to join the high-
way of Jewish justice and Jewish peace ; but this peace and
this justice can achieve complete self-expression, in their
full meaning, neither by revolution nor by class struggle
nor yet by harmonising the interests of nations : for Israel,
a progress of the inner man must reconcile men to Man.

Is this progress possible ? And has this race given the
example of it ?

Alas, Israel is not yet a people of saints ! The Jew knows
his faults and his vices ; he caricatures them to exaggeration
in those " Jewish stories " which he himself hawks round ;
they make him laugh, but they make him suffer, for nothing
is more painful to him, nothing more difficult for him to
pardon, than a Jewish stain on the family honour of Israel.

But with these deformities, which are so often inherited
from the Ghetto and must disappear, has not the Jew
received from the Ghetto itself some beauties, which must
remain ? He has undergone there so much violence, suffered
so much injustice, lived so completely the misery of life,
that pity for the poor and the humiliated has become natural

to him. He has had so long to abstain from shedding blood —even of animals, even of the human beasts who were massacring him—that horror of murder has, as it were, atrophied in him the very motion of killing. And he has seen from so close at hand, in his anguished wanderings, so many men of all races and countries, so many men different everywhere and everywhere alike, that he has understood, that he has felt in the very flesh of his flesh, that Man is One as God is One. So has a race been formed which may have the vices as well as the virtues of other races, but which is assuredly of all races the most *human*.

Look around you and observe : if Christian philanthropy hardly ever embraces Jews, Jewish philanthropy almost always embraces Jews and Christians ; if you can see very flashy Jews everywhere, you will find very few of them in the statistics of homicide ; and even their enemies recognise in them—only, for the matter of that, to censure it—this human sense, which makes of the Jew the instinctive friend of human peace.

Do not misunderstand me, my child. Beyond all doubt Christianity, following Israel, has aimed at spreading, and has in fact spread, the same virtues. It is false to say that it has turned its eyes only to the joys of the beyond, just as it is false to say that Israel has had regard only for this earth. Both, Jew and Christian, believe that, to enter the Kingdom of Heaven, we must strive to establish it here below : the Jew awaits the coming of his Messiah, the Christian awaits the return of his ; and, as I have tried to show in my *Juif du Pape*, in this common waiting lies a common hope.

The human Unity which Israel proclaims, the Church has ceaselessly proclaimed : it is she who, from her very beginning, baptised with the same baptism slave and king ; it is she who, today, enthrones Chinese Bishops, while the lay authorities of civilised States refuse civil equality to the yellow inhabitants of their colonies ; it is she who, by the voice of her great thinkers and her great preachers, denounces in the deformations of nationalism a new form of idolatry ; it was a Pope of the Middle Ages who instituted, in the midst of battles, the Truce of God ; it was a Pope of the twentieth century who pronounced, over a world at war, the loftiest words of peace.

But Israel alone has preserved in its absolute purity the divine message, twofold, of divine Unity and human Unity ; and, on the road that leads to its accomplishment, Israel has taken, by virtue of her history, a step in advance of the rest of mankind, which she must maintain, for all as well as for herself ; for while these ancient truths no longer stir, in so many hearts that have remained pagan, more than a feeble beating, they are, for the Jewish heart, the very blood that makes it beat.

Now at the moment of history when this human sense, heritage of the divine sense and so painfully acquired by Israel, becomes necessary for all the nations, it happens that the Jews, who for so long lived in isolation, have become integrated as citizens in all the nations and behave among them as citizens. They kept themselves apart from all peoples : today they are the only people that includes men of all peoples ; they were a nation among the nations : today they are a League of Nations whose covenant is writ in their blood. Their duty, likewise, is twofold ; and I have learned to understand the two inseparable commandments that dictated my conduct in 1914 : " In every country, be men of your country, even to the sacrifice of your life ; and, at the same time, be Jews ; consecrate to each of your fatherlands the human treasure which is your Jewish heritage ; and the peace of your fatherlands will be your peace, and the peace of men will be your peace." So did Jeremiah teach Israel her task, and so will Israel accomplish it.

But, lost among the nations, might she not risk losing herself ? And losing, with herself, the idea which she has perpetuated ? And so now, at the very hour when humanity begins to feel its unity, at that very hour the return of the Jews to Palestine, bound up, in the words of the prophets, with the miracle of that unity, begins. Dispersed everywhere, Judaism centres itself again in the land of its ancestors ; and the soil which the Zionists recreate there, the language which they relearn there, all the striving of their resurrection, make impossible, for Jews dispersed and for humanity dispersed, the forgetting of Israel and her ideal.

And now, my child, turn to this past, look and reflect. Only one reproach is brought against the Jews, and, in spite of all the lies and all the murders that accompany it, this reproach is justified : they wish to be Jews. Does their past give them the right ? Can it allow anything different ?

See this sublime design, which is revealed at the very beginning and which, from age to age, is realised. Did the Greeks declare to the world in advance that they would show it Beauty ? The Romans, that they would show it Law ? See this people, paltry and sinful, announcing what will be its history at the very beginning of its history ; see it choose the mission which chooses it, and walking with it in the way which it has foretold. See it, this people of eternal sinners, banished twice and surviving two dispersions ; and, as commanded by its prophecies, bringing back from its first exile the divine unity, and preparing, by the second, human unity. See it driven over the face of the earth, always near to dying, and always finding some providential shelter to save it from death. See it bearing its truth, and, to keep it pure, suffering it to spread through the world in the light of the blazing stake. See it, incarnating in its flesh the two loves that torment it, and, at the very moment when it gives itself, with them, to all the nations of the earth, reconstructing, for its own survival still, the home of its memory and its hope, which is the universal hope. And tell me if, in this unique history, you do not feel the eternal presence of a thought and a will which have dictated its task to this people and have made its accomplishment possible, trying it by suffering, saving it in its trials, and guiding it step by step from its grievous past to its triumphant future. For me, my child, who have so long sought the proof of the existence of God—I have found it in the existence of Israel.

I am a Jew because, born of Israel and having lost her, I have felt her live again in me, more living than myself.

I am a Jew because, born of Israel and having regained her, I wish her to live after me, more living than in myself.

I am a Jew because the faith of Israel demands of me no abdication of the mind.

I am a Jew because the faith of Israel requires of me all the devotion of my heart.

I am a Jew because in every place where suffering weeps, the Jew weeps.

I am a Jew because at every time when despair cries out, the Jew hopes.

I am a Jew because the word of Israel is the oldest and the newest.

I am a Jew because the promise of Israel is the universal promise.

I am a Jew because, for Israel, the world is not yet completed : men are completing it.

I am a Jew because, for Israel, Man is not created : men are creating him.

I am a Jew because, above the nations and Israel, Israel places Man and his Unity.

I am a Jew because, above Man, image of the divine Unity, Israel places the divine Unity, and its divinity.

Sometimes, my child, when I wander through a museum, and stand before all the pictures and statues and furniture and armour, the faïence, the crystals, the mosaics, the garments and the finery, the coins and the jewels, gathered there, from every place and every age, to hang on the walls, to stand on the plinths, to line up behind the balustrades, to be classified, numbered and ticketed in the glass cases, I think that one or other of my ancestors may have seen, touched, handled or admired one or other of these things, in the very place where it was made, and at the very time when it was made, for the use, the labour, the pain or the joy of men.

This door with the grey nails, between two poplars, in a gilded frame, this is the Geneva synagogue where my father went in to pray. And see this bridge of boats on the Rhine : my grandfather crossed the Rhine, at Hüningen. And his grandfather, where did he live ? Perhaps as he dreamily calculated the mystical numbers of the Cabbala he saw, through his quiet window, this sledge glide over the snow of Germany or Poland ? And the grandfather of his grandfather's grandfather ? Perhaps he was this money-changer, in this Amsterdam ghetto, painted by Rembrandt.

One of my ancestors may have drunk from this wine goblet, on returning home from the lesson of his master Rashi, at the school of Troyes in Champagne ; one of my ancestors may have sat on this jade-incrusted armchair as he felt a sultan's pulse ; one of my ancestors may have been led to the auto-da-fé by a hooded monk who carried this cross of Castille ; one of my ancestors may have seen his children trampled down by the horse of the Crusader who bore this armour.

These feather head-dresses, did another get them from an American savage ? These African ivories, these Chinese silks, did another buy them by the banks of the Congo or the Amur, to sell them again on the shores of the Ganges or on the Venetian lagoons ?

One of them drove this plough, tempered in the fire, through the plain of Sharon ; one of them went up to the Temple to offer, in these plaited baskets, his tithe of figs.

When this marble Titus was in the flesh, one of my ancestors was dragged bleeding at his chariot wheels in a Roman triumph ; beneath the feet of this bearded mage with the fringed robe, flanked by two winged bulls of human profile, one of my ancestors smelt the dust of Babylon ; at the breath of this porphyry Pharaoh, with the two flat hands on the two flat thighs, one of my ancestors bowed himself down, before girding on his girdle and taking up his staff to follow Moses across the Red Sea ; and this Sumerian idol, with spherical eyes and angular jaws, is perhaps the very one that Abraham broke when he left his Chaldean home to follow the call of his invisible God.

And I say to myself : from this remote father right up to my own father, all these fathers have handed on to me a truth which flowed in their blood, which flows in mine ; and shall I not hand it on, with my blood, to those of my blood ?

Will you take it from me, my child ? Will you hand it on ? Perhaps you will wish to abandon it. If so, let it be for a greater truth, if there is one. I shall not blame you. It will be my fault ; I shall have failed to hand it on as I received it.

But, whether you abandon it or whether you follow it, Israel will journey on to the end of days.

Paris, August-October, 1927.

NOTE

I have translated *école*, where it appears to be used in the sense of "elementary school", simply by "school" and *collège* (an institution of secondary-school rank, not wholly under state-control) by "college": except once, when I have used "school" more vaguely for the whole process of Fleg's education up to the *Ecole normale* stage. I have not attempted to translate *Ecole normale*, which readers will recognise as meaning in this context, not any *école normale* (teachers' training college), but *the Ecole normale* in the *rue d'Ulm*, which takes the cream of French intellectuals by competitive examination and has always turned out not only most of France's University Professors, but many of her most prominent Left-wing politicians. Where I have used the words "the *Ecole*" the reference, of course, is to the *Ecole normale*.

V. G.